Heart Felt Knits

25

Fresh and Modern
Felting Projects

* * * * * *

By Tamara Mello

CHRONICLE BOOKS

SAN FRANCISCO

Library of Congress Cataloging-in-Publication Data:
Mello, Tamara.
    Heart felt knits : 25 fresh and modern felting projects / by Tamara Mello.
      p. cm.
    ISBN 978-1-4521-0252-8
    1. Knitting—Patterns. 2. Felting. 1. Title.
  TT825.M4494 2012
  677.028245—dc23

                                                        2011019124

Manufactured in China

Designed by Ayako Akazawa
Sample Knitting and Pattern Testing by Samantha Fisher
Photo Editing by Jennifer Laski

Photographs by Jessica Sample
Prop styling by Kathryn Kendall
Modeling by Maxime Laski, Gemma Cascardo, Olivia Cascardo, Kathryn Kendall, and Lara Everly

Front cover, Ruffle Scarf, and Cloche Hat photos:
Photographs by Frank W. Ockenfels 3
Hair by John Ruggiero
Makeup by Vanessa Scali
Modeling by Christina Hendricks

Blue Sky Alpacas is a registered trademark of Blue Sky Alpacas, Inc.
Cascade Yarns is a registered trademark of Cascade Yarns, Inc.
Dr. Bronner's Magic Soap is a registered trademark of All-One-God-Faith Inc. Corp.
Lion Brand Yarns and LB Collection are registered trademarks of
Orchard Yarn & Thread Company, Inc.
Naturally Yarn is a registered trademark of Wentworth Distributors NZ Ltd.
Patons is a registered trademark of Patons and Baldwins Limited Co.
Trendsetter Yarn is a registered trademark of Trendsetter Yarns Intl.
Velcro is a registered trademark of Velcro Industries B.V. Corp.

10 9 8 7 6 5 4 3 2

Chronicle Books LLC
680 Second Street
San Francisco, California 94107
www.chroniclebooks.com

For Olivia and Paolo, my two great loves

Contents

* * * * *

Foreword

I met Tamara eight years ago at a party I was hosting. She was the tiny little bird in the corner sipping champagne (although she hardly looked old enough), laughing, smiling, and just being charming. We had a brief conversation, and I floated off to serve more cocktails and refill the cracker plate. To be quite honest, I assumed she was the young date of a friend, and that I would probably never see her again.

But I did see her again, several months later—this time for a mini road trip we were taking to go see a mutual friend perform in a play. We hopped in the car, put on our seat belts, and . . . both pulled out our knitting at the same time! I pulled out one of those shape-changing scarves you make when you first start to knit (due to unintentionally dropping and adding stitches every other row), and she pulled out the most stunning cardigan with a shawl collar. I could tell she was a pro, so I took advantage, and during the next few hours, she helped me fix all the mistakes I had made on my sad little scarf. She also revealed herself to be one of the smartest, wittiest, and warmest people I had ever met.

At one point Tamara asked, "Do you want to start a knitting club with me?" and I was immediately on board. We called some friends that we knew were beginning knitters, and it was on! We named ourselves the "Knitwits." We quickly found out that our name wasn't all that original and that other groups in town had cooler names than us (the "Shizknits," for example), but we didn't care; we were excited and felt that we were creating something special regardless of the name.

Over the next few years, Tamara and I patiently and proudly taught new members to knit and purl, cable, and yarn over. We inspired each other and learned and improved together, but above all—something I hadn't expected going in—we created a new family, because we weren't just knitting together. We were sharing our lives: our accomplishments, our relationships, our family feuds, and our hopes and dreams.

Would I have had a home to stay in when I was unemployed with nowhere to go? Would I have spent summers in Tamara's backyard picking fresh plums, painting my toenails, and sipping white wine? Would I have been in the delivery room for the birth of Tamara and Paolo's beautiful daughter, Olivia? Would I have done any of these things if it weren't for knitting?

I'll never know. But what I do know is that what seemed like a hobby turned out to be much, much more. Knitting is a lifestyle. A community. A group of people who take pride and comfort in creating one little stitch and turning it into something beautiful. Knitting taught me that taking the time to nurture something and make it your own, and ask for help from friends along the way, is what life is all about. And for that, I have Tamara Mello to thank.

Christina Hendricks

* * * * *

Introduction

I grew up in a home where we made stuff. Rainy days meant homemade play dough we could mold, bake in the oven, and paint. My mom was always whipping up elaborately themed birthday parties and gorgeous Halloween costumes fashioned from tulle and tinfoil. My father could build anything. He once made me the world's greatest dollhouse and decorated each room with different wallpaper and carpet. I learned recently that one of my great-grandmothers and her sisters were wool weavers. I suppose my penchant for creating is in the blood.

Working as an actor, as I have for over a decade, one of the first things you learn is that there is a lot of downtime. *A lot.* As it turned out, the endless hours between takes and before auditions ultimately led me to crafting. While I was working on the show *Popular*, my amazing costume designer, Lou Eyrich, taught me the basics of knitting. Once I learned how to knit, I became obsessed, knitting in my trailer, on set, in line at the grocery store, in my car at red lights (not recommended)—anytime I had an extra moment. Knitting was a satisfying way to fill the downtime, and I began to shift more and more focus onto what I was creating with my hands between the duties of my day job.

I quickly learned or taught myself most of the techniques involved in knitting. I admit that felting came a bit later. For a while, my only association with felting was fuzzy, misshapen handbags that did not appeal to me. Then one day, I accidentally washed a little wool hat that I had knit for my daughter, and out of the dryer popped the cutest little felted wool bowl I'd ever seen. And that's all it took. I went into a frenzy, knitting various giant things and then felting them to see what they would become. Many of these early experiments were horrible disasters. But a select few came out well and became the foundation for Blackbird Design House, my online shop.

There are different types of felting techniques. For this book, I focus on the technique of traditional wet felting, which involves knitting with wool yarn to create different shapes and textures and then turning the knitted wool into a felted fabric. Wet felting is an ancient textile process that involves transforming knitted wool into a dense cloth by bonding and shrinking the fibers together using hot water and agitation. Wet felting is by no means an exact science and a lot of experimentation went into developing the patterns for this book. But unpredictability is part of the fun of felting. I also love the idea of using a centuries-old technique to create something that is both modern and timeless.

Felted wool is very dense and water resistant. It is also, amazingly, fire retardant and if protected from moths, virtually indestructible. This makes it the perfect material from which to create something that can be passed down from generation to generation. And because wool is a perfectly renewable, sustainable resource, the practice of knitting and felting is also incredibly eco-friendly. Felting by hand uses very little water and zero electricity yet creates something that can last a lifetime or more. Although felting by machine uses electricity and a bit more water, it results in a lasting and sustainable heirloom. I explain both hand felting and machine felting in the "Felting 101" section; use the technique that works best for you.

The patterns in this book are fairly simple and are written for people with a working knowledge of knitting techniques and terminology. Many of my patterns begin with a simple circle base that is bound off to create a structure for the sides of the piece. I've found that this leads to cleaner lines and an overall sturdier design. I've included at the front of the book a handy Abbreviations guide to help you with the various abbreviations found within each pattern. I've also included a section on Techniques with how-to photos and a helpful Tips, Tools, and Troubleshooting guide just in case you get stuck.

In the following pages, you will find projects that are both practical and whimsical. I hope you find inspiration here and use this book as a jumping-off point to create your own unique pieces. Many of my designs started off as mistakes, which turned into ideas, which turned into something not even remotely resembling what I'd originally intended. That's what I love most about the felting process: It is all about transformation. And really, isn't everything?

Techniques

Felting 101

How to Felt

There are a couple of different ways to achieve a felted look. I prefer the hand felting method. Felting by hand is more work than machine felting, but you ultimately have much more control over how your final product looks. The added bonus is that it is eco-friendly. On the other hand, machine felting is much faster and easier. Try both, and decide which works best for you. One caveat: Machine felting works best in top-loading washers. The front-loading washers don't use as much water or agitation, and you can't stop them in the middle of the cycle to check your progress.

* * * * *

Hand Felting

YOU WILL NEED

Hot water

Ice water

Rubber dishwashing gloves

2 buckets or bowls large enough for the object you're felting

Dr. Bronner's Lavender Liquid Soap (You can really use any liquid soap, but I love this brand because it is all natural and the lavender is a natural moth repellent.)

Small washboard or other textured surface

Stamina

INSTRUCTIONS

Step 1 Place the item to be felted into your container of very hot water. (I usually boil the water on the stove, then add a bit of cold water so I don't scald myself.) Wear gloves and be careful!

Step 2 Add a couple of drops of soap and start agitating, using a spoon, plunger, or other household item, depending on the size of your piece. You can just sort of spin things around so your piece gets thoroughly wet and the wool fibers begin to open up a bit. (You won't see this, but it's happening!) Do this for 5 or 10 minutes to get the felting process started.

Step 3 Remove from hot water, wring out, and plunge into cold water. This process shocks the wool fibers and gets them to open up and start fusing together.

Step 4 Wring out your item gently but thoroughly, and place back in hot water. Begin to scrub your piece against your washboard using the soap as lubrication. Don't use too much soap—just a drop or two—or you won't get the necessary friction. You can scrub your piece alternately against the washboard, against itself, and between your hands. Progress will seem slow at first, but don't give up. You will begin to notice that your wool is looking fuzzy and the stitches less distinct. This is a great sign and means your wool is starting to felt.

Step 5 After a few more minutes, plunge your piece back into the ice water. This will shock the fibers again and cause them to open even more.

Step 6 Gently squeeze out excess water.

Repeat steps 1–6 until the desired amount of felting has occurred. This generally means when you can no longer see the stitches and your knitting looks like a piece of wool fabric. Experiment to find the look that works for you. Some of the patterns in this book are felted less than others, so that you can still see the stitchwork. It really is a matter of personal preference.

Step 7 Rinse.

Step 8 Roll the piece up in a towel to squeeze out excess water.

NOTE:
A salad spinner is another great way to remove excess water from smaller projects. It's like a kinder, gentler spin cycle and really speeds up the drying time. However, I would recommend reserving a salad spinner for this purpose only, or you may end up with some fuzz on your microgreens.

Step 9 Place on mold if required or lay flat to air dry.

NOTE:
Please don't ignore your rubber gloves. Wear them! Most gloves have a textured surface on the palms that's great for felting your fabric, and they really and truly protect your hands from drying out. Take it from me. I ignored my own advice and now have the hands of a one-hundred-year-old washerwoman.

* * * * *

Machine Felting

NOTE:
Again, machine felting should really only be done in a top-loading washing machine, so you can open the door to check on your work. However, if all you have is a front loader and you really don't want to felt by hand, there's a tiny window of time between the wash and rinse cycles when you can open the door. You basically just have to stand there and watch your washer, or you'll miss the window. I still don't advise this method, but it is possible.

Step 1 Place each item to be felted into its own lingerie bag or zippered pillowcase. This is important when felting pieces of different colors to prevent fibers from one color from felting into another. The lingerie bags will also protect your washer pump from getting clogged with fuzz, which can be annoying and expensive!

Step 2 Add a few drops of soap and set the water temperature on the washing machine to hot with a cold rinse. If your model has multiple speeds, set the wash cycle for the longest time with maximum agitation. Add a pair of old jeans or a few tennis balls to the machine to add friction.

Step 3 Check the felting process after five or ten minutes. You can put your item back in to continue felting and start the wash cycle over for more time. Just don't let your machine get to the spin cycle. The spin cycle can cause creases where you don't want them, and they can't be removed. The spin cycle is your *enemy*. Most top-loading machines won't spin or drain when the lid is lifted, which is a helpful feature if you need to step away—you know your knits will be safe. Add a kettle of boiling water if it needs another cycle to keep the water nice and hot. Continue until your item reaches the desired degree of felting. Some people like to be able to still see their stitches while others prefer a more solid fabric. It's really up to you or what your pattern calls for.

Step 4 Once your item is felted to perfection, remove it from the wash. No spin cycle! Many a felted lovely has been beaten beyond recognition in the spin cycle. This is another reason I don't recommend felting in a front loader. They spin to wash rather than agitate.

Step 5 Rinse with cold water and roll up tightly in a towel to squeeze out the excess water.

Step 6 Place on mold if required or lay flat and allow to air dry.

* * * * *

Caring for your felted knits

I recommend spot cleaning with mild soap and cold water when necessary. Should a piece need an all-over cleaning, hand wash it in cold water, reshape, and air dry.

* * * * *

Knitting in the Round

On a Circular Needle

A circular needle is used for creating a tube of knitting. The right side is always facing out, so when you knit every row you are in fact creating stockinette stitch rather than garter stitch. Cast on the desired number of stitches and place a marker after the last stitch (*Figure 1*). Holding the needle with the first cast-on stitch in your left hand and the needle with the last stitch in your right, use the right-hand needle to knit into the first cast-on stitch (*Figure 2*), moving the new stitch off the left and onto the right-hand needle (*Figure 3*). Continue in this manner until you reach your marker. This completes your first round. Continue for desired number of rounds or inches (or centimeters, for those more comfortable with the metric system).

* * * * *

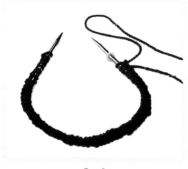

* fig 1 *

* fig 2 *

* fig 3 *

On Double-Pointed Needles (DPNs)

DPNs are used to create knitted tubes of a smaller circumference than circular needles, and in this book I use them to create the circular base for many of my patterns. You will frequently switch from circulars to DPNs while decreasing, when you have too few stitches to continue knitting comfortably on circular needles.

Using four needles, the stitches are arranged in a circle on three of the needles, with the fourth needle used as the working needle. The working needle and the first needle of the round will be worked just as knitting would be done on two needles, with the stitches moving from the left needle onto the working needle. The other two needles just hold the other stitches until they are ready to be worked. Once the first needle's stitches are knitted, the working needle becomes the first needle in the round, and the newly emptied needle becomes the working needle.

To work on double-pointed needles, cast the desired number of stitches onto one of your needles *(Figure 1)*. Divide the stitches evenly among three needles and set a place marker between the last two stitches *(Figure 2)*.

Use the fourth double-pointed needle to join and begin knitting in the round *(Figure 3)*.

* * * * *

* fig 1 *   * fig 2 *   * fig 3 *

Bind-Off Methods

Standard Bind-Off

This is the most common and frequently used bind-off method. Knit the first stitch on your needle, then knit the second stitch. * You now have two stitches on your right-hand needle. Insert the left needle tip into the outside stitch on your right needle *(Figure 1)*, then lift this stitch up and over the second stitch *(Figure 2)* and off your needle. Knit the next stitch, then repeat from * to the end of the row or for the number of stitches required by the pattern. When you have just one stitch remaining on your right needle, break the yarn and pull it through the remaining stitch.

* * * * *

* fig 1 *

* fig 2 *

Three-Needle Bind-Off

Place the stitches to be joined onto two separate needles, and hold them with the right sides of knitting together. Insert a third needle of similar size into the first stitch on each needle and knit them together as one stitch. * Knit the next stitch on the two needles together the same way, then pass the first stitch over the second stitch on the right-hand needle as you do for a standard bind-off. Repeat from * to end of row until you have just one stitch remaining on your right-hand needle. Break yarn and pull tail through the last stitch.

* * * * *

I-Cord

Using two double-pointed needles, cast on the required number of stitches (between 3 and 7). * Without turning the needle, slide stitches to the other side of your needle, pull yarn across the back of your stitches and knit the stitches again. Repeat from * to desired length *(Figure 1)*.

Pick Up and Knit

With the right side facing you, work from right to left. Insert tip of needle into center of stitch below the edge *(Figure 2)*, wrap yarn around needle, and pull it through to make a stitch along the horizontal edge *(Figure 3)*. Pick up one stitch for every stitch in a bound-off or cast-on edge.

NOTE:
For patterns that simply call for you to pick up stitches without knitting them, proceed as follows: With a spare needle and working from left to right, lift up one leg of each stitch along the edge and place them on the needle without knitting them. Then continue with the directions given.

* fig 1 *

* fig 2 *

* fig 3 *

Flat Seam

This is used when you do not want any bulk on the inside of your knitting. You weave in and out of both sides on the very edge of the knitting *(Figure 1)*.

Decreases

Ssk Decrease

This is a left-slanting decrease. Slip two stitches knitwise one at a time onto your right needle *(Figure 2)*. Insert the tip of your left needle from left to right into the front of these two stitches, and knit them together *(Figure 3)*.

* * * * *

* fig 1 *

* fig 2 *

* fig 3 *

K2tog Decrease

This is a right-slanting decrease. Insert the needle into two stitches knitwise, and knit them together as though they were a single stitch (*Figure 1*).

* * * * *

Increases

Kfb Increase

Knit into the front of a stitch but leave it on your left-hand needle (*Figure 2*), knit through the back of the same stitch (*Figure 3*), then slip the original stitch off your needle. You have created two stitches from one.

* * * * *

Yarn Over

Bring the yarn to the front into the purl position, then knit the next stitch. This creates an eyelet and an extra stitch. When you get to the yarn over on the next row, treat it as a regular stitch.

* * * * *

* fig 1 *

* fig 2 *

* fig 3 *

Abbreviations

Italicized terms are described in more detail in the Techniques section.

BO	*bind off*		pfb	purl into front and back of same stitch
C1	color 1		pm	place marker
C2	color 2		psso	pass slip stitch over
CC	contrast color		purlwise	as if to purl
cm	centimeter(s)		rnd(s)	round(s)
CO	cast on		RS	right side
dec	*decrease(s)*		sl	slip
DPN	*double-pointed needle(s)*		*ssk*	*slip, slip, knit*
g	gram(s)		st(s)	stitch(es)
in	inch(es)		tbl	through back loop
inc	*increase(s)*		WS	wrong side
k	knit		yd	yard(s)
k2tog	*knit 2 stitches together*		*yo*	*yarn over*
kfb	*knit into the front and back of the same stitch*		*	repeat starting point
knitwise	as if to knit		*_*	repeat all instructions between asterisks
M1	make one		( )	alternate measurements or instructions
MC	main color			
mm	millimeter(s)		[ ]	instructions that are to be worked as a group a specified number of times
p	purl			
p2tog	purl 2 stitches together			

Tips, Tools, and Troubleshooting

Shrinkage

Felting is by no means an exact science. A general rule of thumb is that most wool will shrink by about 15 percent in width and 25 percent in length. This, however, is a huge generalization. Different types of wool and different blends of wool felt at different rates. Some of the yarns used in this book will shrink up to 50 percent of the original width.

Each of the patterns in this book was written specifically for the yarns called for in each one, but this certainly doesn't mean you can't use different yarn if you want to! Try to use the same weight as the stated yarn so you will get a similar look and feel. Also be sure to do a test swatch to see how the wool felts before using it. I generally knit a 4-by-4-in/10-by-10-cm swatch in stockinette stitch. Check the initial gauge (number of stitches and number of rows over a 2-in/5-cm square) against the gauge given in the pattern instructions. If you have fewer stitches per inch, try using a smaller needle; if you have more stitches per inch, try using a bigger needle. Felt the test swatch and measure the difference in height and width. This will tell you how much the wool shrinks when felted, and you can adjust the pattern accordingly.

Overfelting

You left the work it took you two weeks to knit up in the washing machine too long. The men's size 12 (UK size 11) slipper you intended looks like it might fit an eight-year-old girl. Don't panic! All is not necessarily lost. Felted wool while still wet has amazing stretching capabilities. Pull and stretch that slipper as if your very life depended on it. Use brute force if necessary; I promise it won't rip. Stretch the item over a mold of the appropriate shape and allow to dry. The mold itself doesn't matter as long as it will hold its shape. You can use a bowl, a shoe, a vase, whatever. I've been known to use my own head to stretch out an overfelted hat. Be creative! The felted wool will dry around the mold and retain the new shape.

Mastering Double-Pointed Needles (DPNs)

If you're new to the double-pointed needle and are having trouble, do not despair. There's a definite learning curve with these guys. Review the Techniques section and keep practicing. One of the most obvious problems with DPNs is that the stitches have a tendency to slide off the needles. I use bamboo DPNs almost exclusively. This doesn't eradicate the problem entirely, but it really helps, as they are much less slippery than metal or plastic needles.

Most of the patterns in this book will require you to switch from DPNs to circular needles or vice versa. If it is not specified in the pattern (or even if it is!), switch needles when it is most comfortable for you, for example when you have too few stitches on your circulars or too many on your DPNs to knit comfortably.

There are a couple of other methods for knitting in the round as well. One uses two sets of circular needles rather than DPNs. The other is called the "magic loop" method and uses just one set of circulars. There are loads of tutorials for both of these techniques on the Internet if you are not keen on the idea of using DPNs.

Gauge

In knitting, especially if you're knitting a garment, gauge is incredibly helpful. In felting, however, the rules get a bit skewed. As I've said, it's always a little difficult to know how particular wool is going to felt. I give the gauge of a project when I think it's necessary. If a pattern doesn't have a gauge, don't worry about it; it just isn't all that important.

Mistakes

There are no real mistakes in felting, just future projects waiting to be born. I came up with the idea for the upcycled ornaments because I had a basket full of projects that were either felted too much or just didn't turn out quite right. I wish you a felting career filled only with successful projects. However, if one or two should go awry, save them! Ditto for shrunken or moth-eaten wool sweaters. Turn them into embellishments for hats or patches for jeans, or cut out squares and sew them into a funky patchwork scarf.

Tools and Supplies

These tools are not entirely necessary for the projects in the book, but I find them incredibly helpful.

Row Counter These come in various forms. Some are handheld with a little button on top that you push after each row. Others fit on the end of one of your needles, and you turn a dial after each row. Of course you can just make hash marks on a piece of scrap paper, but I find these to be super helpful.

Stitch Markers These are just little circular pieces of plastic or metal that slide on and off your needles to help you keep track of the stitches in a pattern. They are used frequently when knitting in the round so you know where your round begins and ends. You can also just tie some contrasting scrap yarn in a knot, leaving an opening wide enough for your needle to slide through.

Row Markers These are similar to stitch markers, but have an opening in them so you can attach them directly to a stitch. They don't travel with your needles but stay in one place to mark a certain row you may need to reference later in the pattern. You can use safety pins for the same purpose.

Stitch Holders Stitch holders resemble extra large safety pins and are used for setting aside stitches to be worked later in a pattern. If you just need to mark a few stitches, you can use a safety pin or piece of scrap yarn.

Knit Check This handy little device not only provides a system for checking the size of your needles but also has an inch and centimeter ruler and a row- and stitch-to-the-inch gauge.

Lavender This is a wonderful moth repellent. I felt everything using all-natural lavender soap. I also keep a spray bottle with lavender water in it and occasionally spray it on my felted items to protect them. Plus it smells amazing!

Plastic Bags As hard as I try to use my own shopping bags and not bring home plastic ones, they still manage to sneak into the house. Before recycling them, I use them in my felting. You can cut off the handles to thread through eyelets so they don't become felted shut. You can stuff them inside a bag, slipper, or bangle when machine felting to keep the sides from fusing together. And the same bags can be used over and over again.

Home

01

Nesting Bowls

I love nesting bowls. There's a lovely simplicity to them,
the way they fit together, the way they belong to each other.
Perhaps they remind me of my husband, my daughter, and
myself. I've been collecting vintage English ironstone for
years and for this project, I decided to try to replicate a set
of ironstone nesting bowls in felt. These felted bowls come
in handy for holding paper clips, staples, rubber bands, or
jewelry and other odds and ends. I keep some on a table
in the entryway for keys and meter change. But honestly,
I think they're just pretty sitting all on their own.

* * * * *

Nesting Bowls

GAUGE

6 stitches = 2 in/5 cm, with yarn held double, before felting. Don't go crazy trying to obtain the exact gauge, though; it does not have to be precise. This rule may also be applied to life in general.

YOU WILL NEED

Patons Classic Wool Yarn (100% wool, 223 yd/205 m per 100 g): 1 skein in Winter White (MC) and 1 skein in Natural (CC) *or substitute any worsted weight (#4) 100% wool*

1 set US size 9/5.5 mm DPNs

US size 9/5.5 mm circular needle 16 in/40 cm long, or size to obtain gauge

Stitch marker

Yarn needle

BEFORE YOU BEGIN

Divide each skein of yarn into 2 separate balls so that you can double your yarn.

* * * * *

Small Bowl

With yarn held double and leaving a tail approximately 10 in/25 cm long, cast on 16 stitches with MC to one of your DPNs. Divide the stitches evenly onto 3 needles (5, 5, 6).

FOR THE BOTTOM OF THE BOWL

Place a marker between last 2 stitches. Join to knit in the round, being careful not to twist your stitches.

Round 1 *Kfb, k1, repeat from * to end of round. 24 stitches.

Round 2 (and all even rounds): Knit.

Round 3 *Kfb, k2, repeat from * to end of round. 32 stitches.

Round 5 *Kfb, k3, repeat from * to end of round. 40 stitches.

Round 6 Knit.

Bind off loosely.

FOR THE SIDES OF THE BOWL

Using your circular needle, pick up and knit 40 stitches around the bound-off edge; pm after the last stitch.

Join and knit in the round until the side of your bowl measures 3 in/7.5 cm.

Bind off loosely.

Using your yarn needle, weave in ends. Use the tail from your original cast-on to sew over and close the hole in the bottom of the bowl.

Medium Bowl

FOR THE BOTTOM OF THE BOWL

Rounds 1–6 With CC, follow instructions for small bowl.

Round 7 *Kfb, k4, repeat from * to end of round. 48 stitches.

Round 8 Knit.

Bind off loosely.

FOR THE SIDES OF THE BOWL

Using your circular needle, pick up and knit 48 stitches around the bound-off edge; pm after the last stitch.

Join and knit in the round until the sides of your bowl measure 4 in/10 cm.

Bind off loosely.

Using your yarn needle, weave in ends. Use the tail from your original cast-on to sew over and close the hole in the bottom of the bowl.

Large Bowl

FOR THE BOTTOM OF THE BOWL

Rounds 1-8 With MC, follow instructions for Medium Bowl.

Round 9 *Kfb, k5 repeat from * to end of round. 56 stitches.

Round 10 Knit.

Bind off loosely.

FOR THE SIDES OF THE BOWL

Using your circular needle, pick up and knit 56 stitches around the bound-off edge; pm after the last stitch.

Join and knit in the round until the sides of your bowl measure 5 in/12.5 cm.

Bind off loosely.

Using your yarn needle, weave in ends. Use the tail from your original cast-on to sew over and close the hole in the bottom of the bowl.

Felting

Felt your bowls according to the instructions in the Techniques section. If felting by machine, place each bowl into a separate lingerie bag. Check frequently to avoid any curling around the edges.

Shaping

Once your bowls are felted, it's time to place them on molds. Now don't go all bananas trying to find the perfect mold. I *promise* you have stuff around the house you can use. I use vintage mason jars in 3 different sizes, but you can use any type of jar, can, vase, and so on. You just need 3 molds in similar shapes and graduated sizes to stretch your bowls over until they dry. Bowls should fit snugly against whatever molds you choose, so that the sides and bottom dry straight.

Allow bowls to air dry, remove from molds, and *voilà!* Your nesting bowls are complete.

How to shape bowls on molds.

02

Two-Tone Tray

When my daughter, Olivia, was six months old, she began
getting into everything. And tragically, it became necessary
to baby-proof our home. I am a person who values aesthetics
and craves beautiful surroundings, and this was a fate I was
dreading. My beloved ironstone nesting bowls, beautiful
pinecone collection, and precious silver tray from Argentina
had all become hazards overnight. So I decided to start
making things that were both pleasing to the eye and
safe for tiny, curious hands. This tray was one of my first
experiments in making a container from knitted, felted wool.
It's wonderful for holding remotes or as a stand-alone piece.
Try knitting two in different sizes and nesting them together.

* * * * *

Two-Tone Tray

GAUGE

5½ stitches and 9½ rows = 2 in/5 cm

Does not have to be exact, but close

YOU WILL NEED

Patons Classic Wool Yarn (100% wool; 223 yd/205 m per 100 g):
1 skein each in Lemon Grass (MC) and Dark Gray Mix (CC)
or substitute any worsted weight (#4) 100% wool

US size 10/6 mm circular needle 24 in/60 cm long,
or size to obtain gauge

US size 10/6 mm straight needles (optional)

Stitch marker

Yarn needle

Ribbon or leather cord

Grommet maker and grommets (optional)

BEFORE YOU BEGIN

Divide each skein of your yarn into 2 balls so you
can double your yarn as you knit.

* * * * *

Base of Tray

The base of the tray can be knit on straight needles or back and forth on a circular needle.

Using MC and holding yarn double, CO 21 stitches.

Knit in stockinette stitch for 11 in/28 cm.

Bind off loosely.

Sides of Tray

Using a circular needle and holding CC yarn double, pick up and knit 120 stitches around the rectangle you have just knit: 20 stitches on each short side and 40 stitches on each long side. Don't lose your mind over this little detail. An extra stitch or two on any given side won't kill anyone.

Join and knit in the round for 3 in/7.5 cm.

Bind off.

Weave in ends.

Felting

Felt according to the instructions in the Techniques section.

Shaping

Once your tray is felted, you need something to prop the edges up while it dries. I stick mine in a Pyrex baking dish.

Once it's dry, to keep the edges from drooping you can poke holes in either side of each top corner and thread through some leather or pretty ribbon. You can even use grommets instead of just holes for a more finished look.

03

Round Platter

I originally made this piece to put under a vase as a way to protect my table from moisture. But one day when my mouse pad had gone missing, I grabbed it and it did the trick! It turns out that the little edge around the platter is a perfect place to rest your wrist. You can even roll it up a bit if you want a little more support. This still makes a beautiful platter for small objects or centerpieces; mine just happened to find a permanent home next to my computer.

* * * * *

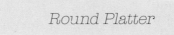
Round Platter

DIMENSIONS

About 12 in/30.5 cm in diameter with a 2-in/5-cm rim

GAUGE

With yarn held double, 6 stitches = 2 in/5 cm

YOU WILL NEED

Patons Classic Wool Yarn (100% wool; 223 yd/205 m per 100 g): 1 skein in Aquarium *or substitute 100 yd/90 m of any worsted weight (#4) 100% wool*

1 set US size 9/5.5 mm DPNs, or size to obtain approximate gauge

US size 9/5.5 mm circular needle 16 in/40 cm long

Stitch marker

Yarn needle

BEFORE YOU BEGIN

Divide yarn into 2 balls so you can double your yarn while knitting.

* * * * *

Base of Platter

You will start knitting on DPNs; switch to a circular needle when it is comfortable to do so.

Holding yarn double, cast on 10 stitches to one of your DPNs, leaving a 10-in/25-cm tail. Divide the stitches over 3 needles (3, 3, 4); pm before your last stitch and join to knit in the round.

Round 1 *Kfb, repeat from * around. 20 stitches.

Round 2 and all even rounds Knit.

Round 3 *Kfb, k1, repeat from * to end. 30 stitches.

Round 5 *Kfb, k2, repeat from * to end. 40 stitches.

Round 7 *Kfb, k3, repeat from * to end. 50 stitches.

Round 9 *Kfb, k4, repeat from * to end. 60 stitches.

Round 11 *Kfb, k5, repeat from * to end. 70 stitches.

Round 13 *Kfb, k6, repeat from * to end. 80 stitches.

Round 15 *Kfb, k7, repeat from * to end. 90 stitches.

Round 17 *Kfb, k8, repeat from * to end. 100 stitches.

Round 19 *Kfb, k9, repeat from * to end. 110 stitches.

Round 21 Bind off loosely.

Sides of Platter

Pick up and knit 110 stitches around the bound-off edge. Place marker and join to knit in the round. Knit 9 rows. Bind off loosely. Using a yarn needle, sew up the hole in the middle using the cast-on tail. Weave in ends.

Felting

Felt according to the instructions in the Techniques section. Rinse in cold water and roll tightly in towel to wring out excess water.

Shaping

I use a large enameled cast-iron pot as the mold for these platters. The weight of the cast iron does a great job flattening the felt to create a smooth surface. You can also use a large flowerpot or just smooth with your hands and straighten the edges. Allow to air dry.

04

Oversize Pencil Holder

This is a bit larger than your average pencil holder. I admit I'm a little OCD about office supplies—I like having tons of sharpened pencils, ballpoint pens, markers, and a few pairs of scissors within arm's reach at all times. This is the perfect pencil holder for creative types who might easily misplace a pencil or two. (As the child of a highly creative mother, I couldn't find a pen or pair of scissors in our house to save my life!) Make this holder to keep on your desk or to give to a creative friend. If you keep it stocked, you may never go hunting for your scissors again.

* * * * *

Oversize Pencil Holder

GAUGE

8 stitches and 10 rows = 2 in/5 cm

YOU WILL NEED

1 empty 16-ounce/1-pint coffee can

Cascade 220 Yarn (100% wool; 220 yd/200 m): 1 skein in color
8401 Gray (MC) and 1 skein in color 9404 Cranberry (CC) *or substitute
100 yd/90 m each in two colors of any worsted weight (#4) 100% wool*

1 set US size 8/5 mm DPNs, or size to obtain gauge

US size 8/5 mm circular needle 16 in/40 cm long

Stitch marker

Yarn needle

* * * * *

Bottom of Holder

Leaving a 10-in/25-cm tail, CO 8 stitches in CC to one of your DPNs.

Divide the stitches evenly among 3 needles (3, 3, 2), pm, and join to knit in the round.

Round 1 *Kfb, repeat from * to end of round. 16 stitches.

Round 2 Knit.

Round 3 *Kfb, k1, repeat from * to end of round. 24 stitches.

Round 4 Knit.

Round 5   Switch to MC and *kfb, k2, repeat from * to end of round. 32 stitches.

Round 6   Knit.

Round 7   *Kfb, k3, repeat from * to end of round. 40 stitches.

Round 8   Knit.

Round 9   *Kfb, k4, repeat from * to end of round. 48 stitches.

Round 10   Knit.

Round 11   *Kfb, k5, repeat from * to end of round. 56 stitches.

Round 12   Knit.

Bind off.

Sides of Holder

With MC and circular needle, pick up and knit 56 stitches around bound-off edge.

Knit in stockinette stitch for 3 in/7.5 cm.

Switch to CC and work even for 4 in/10 cm more.

Switch back to MC and work even for 3 in/7.5 cm more. The sides now measure 10 in/25 cm from the picked-up stitches.

Bind off.

Felting

Felt according to instructions in the Techniques section. Check frequently to be sure the sides of holder don't felt together. Once it is felted, stretch holder over coffee can and air dry. Leave the can in place to provide the structure for your holder and to protect it from sharp points and ink.

05

Knitting Needle Carrier

Knitters tend to accumulate quite a few knitting needles. Non-knitters are always shocked to see just how many needles I have in my stash. What they don't realize is that you often need different sizes and types of needles for a single pattern. The problem is keeping these needles stored, organized, and ready to take on the go. After all, you never know when you'll be stuck in an extra-long line at the bank or post office and have time to dash off a few rows of your latest project. I love this carrier because it stores various sizes of needles and is easy to roll up and stash in your knitting bag before you walk out the door. This makes a great gift for any knitter, but don't forget to make one for yourself!

* * * * *

Knitting Needle Carrier

DIMENSIONS

The final dimensions of the carrier shown are
7 in/18 cm wide by 14 in/36 cm high. Yours may differ
a bit depending on felting time and method.

GAUGE

7 stitches = 2 in/5 cm

YOU WILL NEED

Naturally Yarn Vero (100% wool; 87 yd/80 m per 50 g):
2 skeins in color 77 Moss and Rose *or substitute
any worsted weight (#4) 100% wool*

Commercial felt, about 12 in/30 cm square (I prefer wool
felt to synthetic craft felt. Available in fabric stores.)

US size 9/4.5 mm needles, or size to obtain gauge

10-in/25-cm piece of leather for tie (You can find
leather cord in most craft stores. I used a piece of
suede I upcycled from a thrift store jacket.)

Tailor's chalk or fabric marker

Yarn needle

Sewing machine or sewing needle and coordinating
or contrasting thread

Ruler

* * * * *

For Body of Roll-Up Carrier

CO 63 stitches.

Work even in stockinette stitch until piece measures 13 in/38 cm from cast-on edge, ending with a WS (purl) row.

Bind off.

NOTE:
These are the dimensions for a travel-size carrier. If you would like a wider carrier that holds more needles, just knit more rows before you begin the bind-off. Adjust the length of the tie so it is the same as your new width.

Felting

Felt according to the instructions. This yarn felts up quite quickly, so this carrier is a great project for hand felting.

Lining and Needle Holder

Step 1 Cut a piece of your commercial felt 5 in/13 cm high and ½ in/1.5 cm narrower than your carrier. Mine was 6.5 in/17 cm wide to fit my 7-in-/18-cm-wide carrier. Your width may differ depending on the final dimensions of your carrier.

Step 2 Lay the needle carrier flat with RS down and the tie to one side. Center the piece of commercial felt on the bottom edge of the carrier (the side closest to you) and pin in place along the bottom and sides.

NOTE:
You can choose to have the knit side or the purl side of the carrier be the outside!

Step 3 Using a sewing machine or needle and thread, sew along your pinned edges, leaving a ¼-in/6-mm seam allowance.

Step 4 Using your tailor's chalk or fabric marker and a ruler, draw equidistant vertical lines onto your commercial felt (parallel to the short sides of the carrier). These will be the guidelines for sewing your needle pocket dividers.

NOTE:
See what measurements works best for your fabric width and needles. Mine came out as 1-in/2.5-cm sections. Yours can be anywhere from ¾ in/2 cm to 1.5 in/4 cm each. You can also vary the widths of your sections if you want to accommodate different needle sizes.

Step 5 Using sewing machine or needle and thread, sew straight along guidelines, being sure to backstitch at the pocket openings.

Step 6 Sew leather tie to the center left side of your carrier.

And you're all done. Now just pack up your needles and go!

06

Set of Four Coasters

It always surprises me when someone places a frosty glass, dripping with condensation, on my antique rosewood dining table without a coaster. Heathens! I've spent hours rubbing mayonnaise (it works!) into water rings. And it's for these visitors in particular that I like to keep a stack of felted coasters handy. They are useful and cute, knit up quickly, and absorb lots of moisture. And your guests will be so impressed that your coasters are handmade, they won't even feel awkward when you slide one under their drink.

* * * * *

GAUGE

7 stitches = 2 in/5 cm

YOU WILL NEED

Classic Elite Montera Yarn (50% llama, 50% wool;
127 yd/117 m per 100 g): 1 skein each of Aqua Ice, Majolica Blue,
and Pear *or substitute any worsted weight (#4) 100% wool*

1 set US size 8/5 mm DPNs, or size to obtain gauge

Stitch marker

NOTE:
*The pattern is written for C1 as the center color and C2 as the outer
color. Combine your colors to make as many coasters as you wish.*

* * * * *

Coaster

CO 8 stitches with C1 to one DPN.

Divide stitches evenly among 3 needles (3, 3, 2).

Pm and join to knit in the round.

Round 1 *Kfb, repeat from * around. 16 stitches.

Round 2 and all even rounds Knit.

Round 3 *Kfb, k1, repeat from * to end of round. 24 stitches.

Round 5 *Kfb, k2, repeat from * to end of round. 32 stitches.

Round 7 *Kfb, k3, repeat from * to end of round. 40 stitches.

Round 9 Switch to C2. *Kfb, k4, repeat from * to end of round. 48 stitches.

Round 11 *Kfb, k5, repeat from * to end of round. 56 stitches.

Round 13 *Kfb, k6, repeat from * to end of round. 64 stitches.

Round 15 *Kfb, k7, repeat from * to end of round. 72 stitches.

Round 16 Knit.

Bind off loosely.

Repeat the above instructions for each color combination.

Felting

Felt according to instructions in the Techniques section. This yarn felts quickly and very thickly.

Finishing

Place each coaster under a weight to flatten it. You can use a book, a pot, or anything else with some weight to it. Allow to dry, then use sharp scissors to trim any fuzziness from coasters.

07

Upcycled Ornaments

As you make your way through the wonderful world of felting,
you will undoubtedly stumble a time or two. Things will
felt too much, or felt unevenly, or just turn out a bit wonky.
Whatever happened, don't throw away these odds and ends.
One person's trash is another's Christmas tree ornament!

These ornaments are simple to make and look festive
all year round. If you're itching to try this project before
you've accumulated enough scrap pieces of felt, you
can always knit some up. Just knit a good-size square
and felt it before you start. Or you can find inexpensive
sweaters—alpaca, angora, wool, mohair, and cashmere all
felt beautifully—at a secondhand store. Throw them in the
washing machine on hot, and they will felt right up.

* * * * *

YOU WILL NEED

Fairly large sections, at least 8 by 8 in/20 by 20 cm, of felted wool

Fabric marker

Cookie cutters or other templates in the shape of your choice

Sharp scissors

Ribbon

Needle and thread

Fiberfill

* * * * *

Making Up

Step 1 Using your fabric marker and one of your cookie cutters/templates, trace the image twice onto the felt.

Step 2 Cut out each piece.

Step 3 Cut a 5-in/13-cm length of ribbon.

Step 4 Lay your pieces one on top of the other so that the edges match up.

Step 5 Using a needle and thread, with a loose overcast or blanket stitch, sew your pieces together around the edge, leaving a small opening at the top. The opening should be about twice the width of your ribbon.

Step 6 Stuff your ornament lightly with fiberfill through the opening.

Step 7 Double your ribbon and place the two ends through the opening at the top of the ornament; sew closed.

08

Soft Felted Spheres

Toys today do everything. They light up and play music, they talk, they walk, they fly, they shape-shift. But left to their own devices, children can amuse themselves with a wooden spoon and a piece of string. I wanted to get back to basics with this project. And nothing is more basic than a simple ball. Yet as uncomplicated as it is, its uses are infinite. You can roll it, throw it, and hide it. You can cuddle it, bounce it, and juggle it. You can even introduce it to another ball and make them talk to each other. Plus, these soft spheres look great stacked in a decorative bowl or box.

* * * * *

Soft Felted Spheres

GAUGE

4 stitches = 2 in/5 cm

YOU WILL NEED (FOR THE BALLS AS SHOWN)

Blue Sky Alpacas Bulky Yarn (50% alpaca, 50% wool; 45 yd/41 m per 100 g): 1 skein each of two colors. Grasshopper, Jasmine, Azalea, and Boysenberry are shown. *Or substitute any bulky weight (#6) 100% wool.*

US size 15/10 mm needles, or size to obtain approximate gauge

Yarn needle

Cotton or bamboo fiberfill

NOTE:
You can combine your colors as you please. Just plug your color choices into the pattern as either MC or CC.

* * * * *

For Spheres

Cast on 24 stitches in MC.

Row 1 Knit.

Row 2 Purl.

Rows 3–7 Work even in stockinette stitch.

Row 8 Switch to CC and purl.

Row 9 (K2tog) 12 times. 12 stitches.

Row 10 (P2tog) 6 times. 6 stitches.

Row 11 (K2tog) 3 times. 3 stitches.

Row 12 P3tog.

Break yarn leaving a 10-in/25-cm tail. Thread tail through a yarn needle and pull it through the remaining stitch on your needle. Fold knitting in half and sew up sides to your cast-on row.

NOTE:
You can switch to the MC yarn when appropriate so your seam colors match.

Using your yarn needle, draw yarn through the 24 stitches from your cast-on row. Use the cotton or bamboo stuffing to stuff ball. Pull yarn on needle tightly to gather up stitches. Sew the hole closed and weave in all ends.

Felting

Felt either by hand or machine according to instructions in the Techniques section. When felting is complete, wring out excess water and roll between palms to shape. Air dry.

09

Stuffed Robot

I've always dreamed of having a little girl and sharing with her my doll collection from childhood. When I was four, my grandmother gave me one of my mom's old dolls. She was like an artifact from an ancient time or another world, and I played with her for hours on end. When Olivia was three and a half, I decided it was time to pass my dolls on to her. Giddy with excitement, I dug around the attic until I found the dusty old box containing the holy grail of my girlhood. I presented it to her with a flourish, carefully opening the box to reveal each sacred relic inside and . . . *nothing*. She had no interest in the dolls I had lovingly saved for her. So I made this felted robot for her instead. Luckily, she loves this guy—his bright colors and cuddly size make him the perfect playmate and an eye-catching piece for any kid's room.

* * * * *

Stuffed Robot

GAUGE

8 stitches = 2 in/5 cm

YOU WILL NEED

Cascade 220 Yarn (100% wool, 220 yd/200 m per 100 g): 2 skeins
in Aqua (MC), 1 skein in Purple (CC1), 1 skein in Orange (CC2)
or substitute any worsted weight (#4) 100% wool yarn

US size 9/5.5 mm straight needles, or size to obtain gauge

1 set US size 9/5.5 mm DPNs

Yarn needle

Bamboo or polyester fiberfill

* * * * *

For Body of Robot

TOP

Using MC and straight needles, cast on 25 stitches.

Work even in stockinette stitch for 24 rows.

Bind off loosely.

SIDE 1

Pick up and knit 25 stitches along bound-off edge of top.

Work in stockinette stitch for 49 rows.

Bind off loosely.

BOTTOM

Pick up and knit 25 stitches along bound-off edge of side 1.

Work in stockinette stitch for 24 rows.

Bind off loosely.

SIDE 2

Pick up and knit 25 stitches along bound-off edge of bottom.

Work in stockinette stitch for 49 rows.

Leave stitches on needle.

Using second needle, pick up 25 stitches along your original cast-on edge.

Connect the 25 picked-up stitches from the cast-on edge and the 25 stitches from side 2 using the three-needle bind-off method. (See Techniques section.)

Front of Robot

Pick up and knit 25 stitches along one edge of the top. (The top and bottom are the same, so either will do.)

Work in stockinette stitch for 49 rows.

Leave stitches on needle.

Using second needle, pick up 25 stitches along the edge of the bottom that's facing you.

Connect the 25 picked-up stitches and the 25 stitches from the front using the three-needle bind-off method. (See Techniques section.)

Using the yarn needle and a loose overcast stitch, sew up sides of robot.

Back of Robot

Work the same as for the front, leaving a 2-in/5-cm opening along one side seam.

You will use this opening after felting to add stuffing to your robot.

Arms (make 2)

Using CC1, cast on 20 stitches.

Knit 10 rows in garter stitch.

Switch to MC and continue in garter stitch for 6 rows.

Switch to CC2 and continue in garter stitch for 12 rows.

Bind off.

Fold in half lengthwise, then fold in half again.

The extra bulk in the arms will give them some stability so they stick out from the robot's body.

Using yarn needle, sew the two short ends and the open side closed, changing yarn color to match as you go.

Sew one end of each arm to center sides of robot body.

Legs (make 2)

Using CC1, cast on 20 stitches.

Knit 12 rows in garter stitch.

Switch to MC and continue in garter stitch for 8 rows.

Switch to CC2 and continue in garter stitch for 14 rows.

Bind off.

Fold in half lengthwise, then in half again.

Using yarn needle, sew the two short ends and the open side closed, changing yarn color to match as you go.

Sew ends of legs onto center bottom of robot body.

Antenna

Using CC2, cast on 4 stitches to DPN.

Work I-cord for 4 in/10 cm. (See Techniques section.)

Bind off.

Sew to top of robot.

Mouth

Using straight needles and CC1, cast on 15 stitches.

Knit 8 rows in garter stitch.

Bind off.

Weave in ends.

Eyes (make 2)

Using DPNs and CC2, cast on 4 stitches.

Divide among 3 needles (1, 1, 2).

Kfb in each stitch. 8 stitches.

Pm and join to knit in the round.

Round 1 Knit.

Round 2 Switch to CC1 and *kfb, k1, repeat from * to end of round. 12 stitches.

Round 3 Knit.

Round 4 *kfb, k2, repeat from * to end of round. 16 stitches.

Round 5 Knit.

Bind off and weave in ends.

Felting

If felting your robot in the washing machine, stuff him loosely with plastic bags. (It's a great way to reuse grocery bags, and they will last for several projects.) This will keep the sides from felting together.

Felt eyes and mouth by placing them in their own lingerie bag or pillowcase. They will be sewn to your robot after felting.

Felt until you've achieved the shape you want. If you want a more rectangular shape, then felt your robot less. A longer felting time will result in rounder, less defined edges, giving your robot more of a ball shape.

Finishing

Using a loose overcast stitch in matching colors, sew eyes and mouth to the front of your robot.

Stuff robot and sew up seam opening with a sharp yarn needle.

10

Little Acorns

My daughter and I love collecting acorns at her grandparents'
house in Florida. We've spent hours crawling around together
beneath the trees as we gather up our treasures, and we've
decided that fairies must surely use the acorn caps for hats.

We keep these felt acorns nestled in a felted bowl next
to our fireplace. They're lovely to look at and to hold and
make a perfect seasonal decoration for autumn.

* * * * *

Little Acorns

GAUGE

Approximately 10 stitches = 2 in/5 cm

While the gauge is not critical for this project, be sure to use a needle size appropriate for your yarn.

YOU WILL NEED

Worsted weight wool scrap yarn

US size 7/4.5 mm needles

Yarn needle

Glue gun or craft glue

Clean acorn caps (If you can't find your own, they're readily available for purchase online.)

* * * * *

Knitting

Cast on 8 stitches. Leave a 20-in/50-cm tail.

Rows 1–3 Work in stockinette stitch.

Row 4 (P2tog) 4 times. 4 stitches.

Row 5 (K2tog) twice. 2 stitches.

Row 6 P2tog. 1 stitch.

Break yarn leaving a 12-in/30-cm tail. Thread tail through a yarn needle and pull it through the remaining stitch on your needle. Fold knitting in half and sew up sides, working up to your cast-on row. Using your yarn needle, pick up the 8 stitches you cast on. Stuff original tail into the center of ball and pull yarn on needle tightly to gather up stitches. Sew the hole closed and weave in the end.

Felting

These felt quickly and easily by hand but can certainly be done in the machine as well. The key is to roll the ball between your palms while still wet in order to make it as round as possible. Allow to dry.

Finishing

Use a glue gun to glue the felted balls into the acorn caps. If you like, you can drill a tiny hole through the top of the cap first and thread a piece of ribbon or embroidery floss through so the acorn can be hung.

11

Baby Elf Booties

It is my belief that while babies are tiny and unable to voice their opinions, they should wear the absolutely most adorable, whimsical clothing possible. I loved dressing my daughter, Olivia, when she was a baby. Now she insists on dressing herself, so I encourage you to take advantage of the baby window while you have it! The Baby Elf Booties are soft, cozy, and irresistible slippers for your little one. Or knit up a pair as a memorable baby shower gift.

* * * * *

SIZING

3–6 months (6–12 months)

Instructions for 2 sizes are given here. Much of the sizing can also be determined by how little or how much you felt the booties.

GAUGE

8 stitches and 10 rows = 2 in/5 cm

YOU WILL NEED

Patons Classic Wool Yarn (100% wool; 210 yd/194 m per 100 g):
1 skein in Currant (MC) and 1 skein in Wisteria (CC) *or substitute 120 yd/110 m of other worsted weight (#4) 100% wool*

US size 8/5 mm straight needles, or size to obtain gauge

1 set US size 8/5 mm DPNs

Yarn needle

* * * * *

Heel

Using straight needles, cast on 3 (5) stitches in MC.

Row 1 Knit.

Row 2 Kfb, k to last stitch, kfb.

Row 3 Purl.

Row 4 Kfb, k to last stitch, kfb.

Row 5 Purl.

Row 6 Kfb, k to last stitch, kfb.

Row 7 Purl.

Row 8 Kfb, k to last stitch, kfb. 11 (13) stitches.

Row 9 Purl.

*The following extra rows are for the 6-12 month size **only**.*

Extra Row 1 *Kfb, k to last stitch, kfb.*

Extra Row 2 *Purl. 15 stitches.*

Row 10 (all sizes) Knit.

Row 11 Purl.

Break yarn and leave stitches on needle.

Foot

With right side facing and MC, starting at the point of the heel triangle, use first DPN to pick up and knit 9 (10) stitches along the right side; with second DPN, knit the 11 (15) stitches held on the needle; with third DPN, pick up and knit 9 (10) stitches down the left side of the heel. 29 (35) stitches.

Turn work; do not join to knit in the round. You will be working back and forth across the three needles as follows:

Row 1 (WS) Purl. Turn.

Row 2 K9 (10), slip1, k9 (13), slip1, k to end of row. Turn.

Repeat the last 2 rows until bootie measures 4 in/10 cm from the pick-up row.

Place detachable markers on the first and last stitch of your last row.

Repeat Rows 1 and 2 above for another 1 in/2.5 cm (1.5 in/4 cm), ending with a purl row.

Shaping Toe

NOTE:
At this point you may find it easier to switch back to straight needles.

Row 1 K5 (7), slip1, k1, psso, k2tog, k11 (13), slip1, k1, psso, k2tog, k5 (7). 25 (31) stitches.

Row 2 and all even rows Purl.

Row 3 K4 (6), slip1, K1, psso, k2tog, k9 (11), slip1, k1, psso, k2tog, k4 (6). 21 (27) stitches.

Row 5 K3 (5), slip1, k1, psso, k2tog, k7 (9), slip1, k1, psso, k2tog, k3 (5). 17 (23) stitches.

Row 7 K2 (4), slip1, k1, psso, k2tog, k5 (7), slip1, k1, psso, k2tog, k2 (4). 13 (19) stitches.

Row 9 K1 (3), slip1, k1, psso, k2tog, k3 (5), slip1, k1, psso, k2tog, k1 (3). 9 (15) stitches.

Row 11 K1 (2), slip1, k1, psso, k2tog, k0 (3) slip1, k1 psso, k2tog, k0 (2). 5 (11) stitches.

*The following extra 2 rows are for the 6-12 month size **only**.*

Extra Row 1 *Purl.*

Extra Row 2 *(Slip1, k1, psso) 2 times, k2tog, k1, (k2tog) 2 times. 6 stitches.*

Row 12 (all sizes) Purl.

Bind off.

Cut yarn leaving a 16-in/40-cm tail, pull through remaining stitch on needle, and secure. Sew instep from point of toe to markers using a flat seam. Remove markers.

Cuff

With the right side facing, beginning at front seam, use CC and DPNs to pick up and knit 36 stitches around the opening of bootie. Divide stitches onto three needles.

Do not join to knit in the round. Turn work and knit back and forth across needles as follows:

Row 1 K36, turn.

The next 2 rows will create the eyelets for your laces.

Row 2 K2tog, yo, k2tog, k to last 4 stitches, k2tog, yo, k2tog. 32 stitches.

Row 3 K1, (k1, p1) in the yo, k to last 2 stitches, (k1, p1) in the yo, k1. 36 stitches.

Row 4 Knit.

Continue even in garter stitch (knit every row) until cuff measures 2 in/5 cm.

I-Cord Laces (make 2)

With CC, cast on 2 stitches to DPN. Follow the I-cord instructions in the Techniques section and make a 10-in/25-cm I-cord.

Finishing

Weave in all ends neatly. Cut the handles from a plastic grocery bag or use a piece of cotton waste yarn to thread through the eyelets on either side of your cuff. Tie in a knot. These will keep your eyelets open during felting and can be cut off once felting is complete.

Felting

Felt according to the instructions in the Techniques section. I recommend felting your I-cords by hand. They felt up quickly and have a tendency to tangle in the washing machine. Whether felting by machine or by hand, turn the booties inside out and back a few times to insure even felting. Once they are felted, thread the I-cords through your eyelets and stuff the booties with plastic bags to shape and dry.

NOTE:
If you're making these for a child that is already walking, be sure to attach a non-slip material (like the kind sold in fabric stores for pajama feet) to the soles. Another solution is to use a hot glue gun and just make some squiggly lines across the bottom of the sole, then allow to dry. This provides great traction and is super easy.

12

Men's Clog Slippers

My wonderful husband, Paolo, loves slippers. He had a pair of store-bought clog slippers that he completely wore out, so I decided to try to copy them. After all, he puts up with a lot from me—yarn everywhere, my head always in a knitting project. It was time to make the man a pair of slippers.

I wanted something that could be knit up on one set of circular needles because I travel a lot with my knitting, and knitting on double-pointed needles, as you normally would for slippers or socks, can be difficult when you want to just pick up and go. After many failed attempts, I came up with this design (for which you only need the double-pointed needles on the last few rows). The wonderful husband may still be saddled with me, but at least his feet are warm!

* * * * *

Men's Clog Slippers

SIZING

Men's shoe size 8-10 (or 11-13) / 7-9 (or 10-12)
Much of the sizing can be determined in the felting process.

GAUGE

6 stitches = 2 in/5 cm with yarn held double

YOU WILL NEED

Lion Brand Fishermon's Wool Yarn (100% wool; 465 yd/425 m per
8 oz): 1 skein in Oatmeal (MC) and 1 skein in Natural (CC)

US size 13/9 mm circular needle 16 in/40 cm long,
or size to obtain gauge

Stitch markers

1 set US size 13/9 mm DPNs

Yarn needle

* * * * *

Heel

Divide each yarn skein into 2 separate balls so you can double your yarn while knitting. Make both slippers the same.

Using CC held double and circular needle, cast on 40 stitches. Place marker and join to knit in the round.

Round 1 Knit.

Round 2 K11, place marker, k18, place marker, and turn work.

NOTE:
You will knit back and forth across these 18 stitches for several rows to create the heel of your clog.

Heel Flap

With wrong side facing, switch to MC.

Row 1 Slip1, purl to marker, turn.

Row 2 Slip1, k to marker, turn.

Repeat these 2 rows 5 (6) times, then repeat Row 1 once more.

Shaping Heel

Row 1 Slip1, k9, ssk, k1, turn, leaving 5 stitches unworked.

Row 2 Slip1, p3, p2tog, p1, turn, leaving 5 stitches unworked.

Row 3 Slip1, k4, ssk, k1, turn, leaving 3 stitches unworked.

Row 4 Slip1, p5, p2tog, p1, turn, leaving 3 stitches unworked.

Row 5 Slip1, k6, ssk, k1, turn, leaving 1 stitch unworked.

Row 6 Slip1, p7, p2tog, p1, turn, leaving 1 stitch unworked.

Row 7 Sl1, k8, ssk, turn.

Row 8 P9, p2tog, turn.

You now have 10 heel stitches.

NOTE:
Your heel markers will have fallen off by now, but you no longer need them.

Gusset

You will now continue knitting in the round.

Round 1 With right side facing, k5, pm (this new marker at the center of the heel marks the new beginning of the round), k5, pick up and knit 12 (13) stitches along side of heel flap, k the 22 stitches of the cuff (removing original marker as you go), pick up and knit 12 (13) stitches down second side of heel flap, k5. 56 (58) stitches.

Round 2 and all even rounds Knit.

For larger size only, work the following extra 2 rows.

Extra Round 1 *K6, k2tog, k22, ssk, k16.*

Extra Round 2 *Knit.*

Round 3 (all sizes) K15, k2tog, k22, ssk, k15.

Round 5 K14, k2tog, k22, ssk, k14.

Round 7 K13, k2tog, k22, ssk, k13. 50 stitches.

Round 9 K12, k2tog, k22, ssk, k12.

Round 11 K11, k2tog, k22, ssk, k11.

Round 13 K10, k2tog, k22, ssk, k10.

Round 15 K9, k2tog, k22, ssk, k9.

Round 17 K8, k2tog, k22, ssk, k8. 40 stitches.

Foot

Work even in rounds until clog measures 12 (14) in/30 (40) cm from back of heel.

DECREASE FOR TOE

Round 1 *K6, k2tog, repeat from * to end of round. 35 stitches.

Round 2 and all even rows Knit.

Round 3 *K5, k2tog, repeat from * to end of round. 30 stitches.

Switch to DPNs and divide stitches evenly on 3 needles (10 stitches per needle). Place marker and continue knitting in the round.

Round 5 *K4, k2tog, repeat from * to end of round. 25 stitches.

Round 7 *K3, k2tog, repeat from * to end of round. 20 stitches.

Round 9 *K2, k2tog, repeat from * to end of round. 15 stitches.

Round 11 *K1, k2tog, repeat from * to end of round. 10 stitches.

Round 13 *K2tog, repeat from * to end of round. 5 stitches.

Finishing

Cut yarn leaving a 12-in/30-cm tail. Using a yarn needle, draw the tail through the remaining 5 stitches. Fasten off and weave in all ends on wrong side of clog.

Felting

As with most of your larger pieces, it's much easier and faster to felt these in the washing machine. The sizing can be largely be controlled by how much you felt your slipper.

Shaping

The easiest way to dry and mold your clogs will be to stretch them over a shoe in the desired size. When I made these for my husband I used one of his Converse™ tennis shoes as the mold, and they worked great.

NOTE:

Clogs can be worn as is or you can add a sole to them. You can find ready-made soles in most craft stores or you can make your own. I've used suede or leather jackets bought cheaply at secondhand stores. Just trace the shape of your clog onto the leather, cut out, and sew to the bottom of clog using a sewing needle and thread and a blanket stitch.

Style

13

Chain Necklace

I love using felt to create something unexpected, and because I'm also a jewelry designer, a necklace seemed like a great choice. I was drawn to the idea of replicating the links of a chain for this project—I liked the thought of taking something that would ordinarily be made of cold, hard metal and making it from something soft and warm. This sort of contrast really inspires my work.

This piece makes a bold statement paired with a little black dress. But, more often than not I throw it on with jeans and a T-shirt for a look that's casual yet pulled together. It works well as a statement necklace or ultra-cozy warm scarf. Warning: People tend to ask about it, so don't wear it if you aren't in the mood to chat!

* * * * *

Chain Necklace

YOU WILL NEED

Patons Classic Wool Yarn (100% wool; 223 yd/205 m per 100 g):
1 skein each in Dark Gray (MC), Black (CC1), and Red (CC2)
or substitute any worsted weight (#4) 100% wool

US size 9/5.5 mm circular needle 9 in/23 cm long

Stitch marker

Yarn needle

NOTE:
If you don't have a 9-in/23-cm circular needle, use DPNs.

* * * * *

First Link

Divide each skein of yarn in half so you have 2 balls of each color and can double your yarn.

With MC and holding yarn double, CO 55 stitches, pm, and join to knit in the round.

Knit even for 10 rows.

Bind off.

You now have a circle. Set it aside.

Small Link

CO 30 stitches with CC1 held double.

Before you start to knit, take your first link and put it onto your circular needle (*see Figure 1*), pm, and join to knit in the round.

Knit 10 rows.

Bind off.

You now have the first two links of your chain.

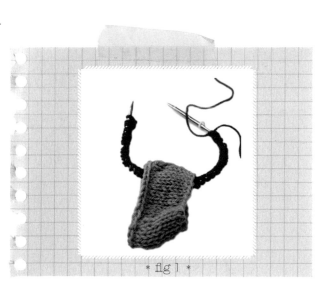

* fig 1 *

Large Link

CO 55 stitches with MC held double.

Place the link you just finished onto your needle as before, pm, and join to knit in the round.

Knit 10 rows.

Bind off.

NOTE:

Do not, I repeat, do not forget to loop the last finished link through the new one before you join your stitches. I've done this more times than I care to remember, and it infuriates me every time. You just end up with a lonely, unjoined circle.

Continue in this manner, alternating colors and sizes, until you have 9 links.

Joining the Ends

CO 30 stitches with CC2 held double for your final link.

Take the first and last links of your chain and put them onto your needles, pm, and join to knit in the round.

Knit 10 rows.

Bind off.

Weave in all ends with yarn needle.

NOTE:

The sides of each link will curl in. Let them. They will felt together and create a seam.

Felting

Felt according to instructions in the Techniques section. Lay on a flat surface to dry. Amaze your friends.

14

Farmers' Market Tote

This bag makes me happy. It holds everything! I use it
for groceries, gym clothes, library books, anything. It's
utilitarian *and* pretty. Best of all, it isn't plastic, so it won't
end up damaging the environment by sitting in a landfill.
It is durable and will last for years. This bag is one of
my personal favorites and goes with me everywhere.
Make one for yourself and all your friends!

* * * * *

Farmers' Market Tote

DIMENSIONS

Before felting: 22 in/56 cm wide and 28 in/71 cm tall

After felting: approximately 10.5 in/45.8 cm wide and 14 in/35.6 cm tall

GAUGE

7 stitches and 10 rows = 2 in/5 cm

YOU WILL NEED

Lion Brand LB Collection Organic Wool Yarn (100% wool;
185 yd/170 m per 100 g): 2 skeins in Eggplant (MC) and 2 skeins in
Avocado (CC) *or substitute any worsted weight (#4) 100% wool*

NOTE:

*This particular yarn shrinks a great deal in length when
felted. If using a different yarn, be sure to do a swatch
test to determine the correct measurements.*

1 set of leather purse handles

1 set US size 9/5.5 mm DPNs, or size to obtain gauge

US size 9/5.5 mm circular needle 24 in/60 cm long

Yarn needle

* * * * *

Bottom of Bag

CO 10 stitches with MC to one DPN, leaving a 10-in/25-cm tail. Divide the stitches over three needles (3, 3, 4); pm before your last stitch, and join to knit in the round. Switch to a circular needle when it's no longer comfortable to knit on DPNs.

Round 1 *Kfb, repeat from * around. 20 stitches.

Round 2 and all even rows Knit.

Round 3 *Kfb, k1, repeat from * to end. 30 stitches.

Round 5 *Kfb, k2, repeat from * to end. 40 stitches.

Round 7 *Kfb, k3, repeat from * to end. 50 stitches.

Round 9 *Kfb, k4, repeat from * to end. 60 stitches.

Round 11 *Kfb, k5, repeat from * to end. 70 stitches.

Round 13 *Kfb k6, repeat from * to end. 80 stitches.

Round 15 *Kfb, k7, repeat from * to end. 90 stitches.

Round 17 *Kfb, k8, repeat from * to end. 100 stitches.

Round 19 *Kfb, k9, repeat from * to end. 110 stitches.

Round 21 *Kfb, k10, repeat from * to end. 120 stitches.

Round 23 *Kfb, k11, repeat from * to end. 130 stitches.

Round 25 *Kfb, k12, repeat from * to end. 140 stitches.

Round 27 *Kfb, k13, repeat from * to end. 150 stitches.

Round 29 *Kfb, k14, repeat from * to end. 160 stitches.

Round 30 Knit.

Bind off loosely.

This is the round bottom of your bucket-shaped bag. Using a yarn needle, sew up the hole in the middle using the cast-on tail. Weave in ends.

Body of Bag

Using a circular needle and MC, pick up and knit 160 stitches around the bound-off edge. Pm and join to knit in the round.

Work even in stockinette stitch for 20 rounds.

Switch to CC and knit 20 rounds.

Repeat the last 40 rounds 2 times more. The bag measures approximately 28 in/65 cm.

Bind off loosely.

You have a gigantic bag, but don't worry; it will felt down to a beautiful, sturdy tote.

Weave in ends.

Felting

Felt according to instructions in the Techniques section. For a piece this size, it is definitely easier to felt by machine, but keep close watch so the top edge doesn't curl.

Shaping

Stuff your bag with a large towel so that the sides are straight and the bag can sit up on its own. Allow to air dry.

Finishing

Using a yarn needle and matching yarn, sew the handles to the top of your bag.

15

Ruffle Scarf

I love this piece for its sheer drama; people can't help but take a second look at it. The ruffles remind me of an Elizabethan collar. I think it's important for functional garments to still make you feel beautiful while you wear them. This piece is pretty and also incredibly warm and water resistant. You can wrap this scarf once or several times, and it frames the face beautifully.

* * * * *

Ruffle Scarf

GAUGE

6 stitches and 6½ rows = 2 in/5 cm

YOU WILL NEED

Cascade Jewel Hand Dyed Yarn (100% wool; 142 yd/131 m per 100 g):
2 skeins in Color 9992 (MC) and 3 skeins in Color 8422 (CC)
or substitute any chunky weight (#5) 100% wool

US size 10/6 mm straight needles, or size to obtain approximate gauge

US size 10/6 mm circular needle 60 in/150 cm long

NOTE:
*If you can't find a 60-in/150-cm circular needle, you
can also use 2 sets of 32-in/80-cm needles.*

Stitch marker

Yarn needle

* * * * *

Body of Scarf

Using straight needles, CO 24 stitches with MC.

Work even in stockinette stitch for 79 in/178 cm.

Bind off loosely.

Ruffle

Round 1 with CC Pick up and knit 518 stitches around perimeter of scarf: 22 stitches on each short end and 237 stitches on each long side. Place a marker and join to knit in the round.

Round 2 and all even rounds Knit.

Round 3 *K1, kfb repeat from * to end. 777 stitches.

Round 5 *K1, kfb repeat from * to end. 1,166 stitches.

Round 7 *K1, kfb repeat from * to last stitch, k1. 1,749 stitches.

Round 8 Knit.

Round 9 Bind off loosely.

Felting

In order to keep some pliability and movement in your wrap, you need to felt it only very lightly. Felt until the spaces between your stitches begin to disappear but not so much that the fabric becomes stiff. Lay flat to dry.

16

Laptop Messenger Bag

I needed a bag that could hold my laptop when I traveled. It was important to me to have something that was padded enough to protect my computer but that still looked fashionable. Everything I saw in stores just looked like a computer bag— boring and too similar to everyone else's. So I decided to make my own. This bag is roomy enough to hold your computer, cell phone, and other essentials but doesn't feel bulky or cumbersome. It opens easily, so taking your computer in and out at airports is a cinch, but the magnetic closure keeps it shut when you need it to. Felted wool is naturally water repellent, so it will keep your laptop cozy and dry. I think the look is handsome enough for a man to carry, too.

* * * * *

Laptop Messenger Bag

NOTE:

I have not had any problems with the magnetic closure and my laptop, but use at your own risk. If you opt out of the magnet, try a nice button or Velcro strip instead.

GAUGE

6 stitches and 8 rows = 2 in/5 cm with yarn held double

YOU WILL NEED

Lion Brand Fishermen's Wool Yarn (100% wool; 465 yd/425 m per 8 oz): 1 skein in Nature's Brown (MC) and 1 skein in Brown Heather (CC) *or substitute any worsted weight (#4) 100% wool*

US size 10/6 mm needles, or size to obtain gauge

Yarn needle

Two 1½-in/38-mm metal rings

One ¾-in/18-mm magnetic snap

Decorative button

BEFORE YOU BEGIN

Divide each skein of yarn into 2 balls so you can double your yarn.

* * * * *

Bottom of Bag

With MC held double, CO 47 stitches.

Work in stockinette stitch for 4 in/10 cm.

Bind off.

Front of Bag

With CC held double and RS facing, pick up and knit 47 stitches along the edge you just bound off.

Work even in stockinette stitch until piece measures 13 in/33 cm from the picked-up stitches.

Bind off.

Back of Bag

With CC held double and RS facing, pick up and knit 47 stitches along the original cast-on edge. (This is the long edge opposite the piece you just finished.)

Work even in stockinette stitch until piece measures 13 in/33 cm from the picked-up stitches.

Bind off.

Sides

With MC held double and RS facing, pick up and knit 12 stitches along one of the short sides of the bottom rectangle.

Work even until piece measures 13 in/33 cm from the picked-up stitches.

Bind off.

Work the second side the same way.

The bottom and the four sides of the bag are now complete. Sew the edges of each side to the front and back panels along the 13-in/33-cm sides.

Top Flap

With MC held double and RS facing, pick up and knit 47 stitches along the top edge of the back panel.

Work even in stockinette stitch for 13 in/33 cm.

Bind off.

Bases for Strap

With MC held double and RS facing, pick up and knit 10 stitches, centered, from the top of one side panel.

Work even in stockinette stitch for 6 in/15 cm.

Bind off, leaving a 10-in/25-cm tail.

Insert this piece through one of your metal rings and double it over with wrong sides together.

Thread tail onto the yarn needle and sew the bound-off edge to the inside of edge of side panel.

Repeat on the opposite side to attach the second ring.

Strap

With MC held double, CO 10 stitches.

Work even in stockinette stitch for 42 in/107 cm.

Bind off, leaving a 10-in/25-cm tail.

Thread the bound-off end of the strap approximately 2 in/5 cm through one metal ring and fold it over with wrong sides together. Remember, the right side of the strap should face out. Use the tail to sew the bound-off end to the wrong side of the strap about 2 in/5 cm above the ring.

Being sure not to twist the strap, repeat with the cast-on end and the opposite metal ring.

Cell Phone Pocket

With MC held double, CO 24 stitches.

Work even in stockinette stitch until piece measures 7 in/18 cm.

Bind off.

Center the pocket on the inside of the back panel. Using the yarn needle, sew the sides and bottom of your pocket to the back panel. Place a piece of plastic bag in the cell phone pocket prior to felting to keep it from attaching to the back panel. Just be sure not to overstretch the pocket or your bag won't felt properly. I learned this the hard way and my first bag had a big, unfelted lump in the back. Not pretty.

Felting

Felt according to instructions in the Techniques section. If felting by machine check frequently to ensure the top edge doesn't curl, the strap remains straight, and the pocket doesn't become felted to the back panel.

Lay flat to dry, allowing strap to hang off side of table so it dries straight.

Finishing

Attach metal snap pieces to the outside of the front panel and the inside of the flap.

Sew button on outside flap over the snap.

17

Mini Cashmere Clutch

I adore a giant, oversize handbag. On any given day I'm
carrying around knitting projects, spare clothes for Olivia,
snacks, my laptop, and maybe a small dog. With all this
happening in one purse, it's very important to have smaller
compartments to store things and stay (somewhat) organized.
This little bag is great for stashing lipstick, credit cards, ID,
and a cell phone. You can even use it as a sunglasses case.
Throw it in a larger bag or carry it on its own for a night on the
town. I knit this up in cashmere for an extra touch of luxury,
but feel free to experiment with other fibers and textures.

* * * * *

Mini Cashmere Clutch

GAUGE

8 stitches and 9 rows = 2 in/5 cm

YOU WILL NEED

Trendsetter Kashmir Yarn (65% cashmere, 35% silk; 110 yd/100 m = 50 g):
1 skein in Gray *or substitute similar worsted weight (#4)*
cashmere blend yarn

US size 7/4.5 mm needles, or size to obtain gauge

Stitch holder

1 set US size 7/4.5 mm DPNs

Yarn needle

One ½-in/1.3-cm button

* * * * *

Front

Cast on 40 stitches.

Row 1 Knit.

Row 2 Purl.

Rows 3–18 Work even in stockinette stitch.

Row 19 K19, slip next 2 stitches to stitch holder, k19.

NOTE:
Just leave the stitches on the holder at the front of your work. You will use them later to make the I cord tie.

Row 20 P19, M1 purlwise, M1 purlwise, p19. 40 stitches.

Rows 21–27 Work 7 more rows in stockinette stitch, ending with a knit row.

Bind off, keeping last stitch on needle. Do not break yarn.

Turn the work, keeping the remaining stitch on the right-hand needle.

Bottom

With the last stitch of the front on your needle, pick up and knit 39 stitches along the bound-off edge. 40 stitches.

Row 1 Purl.

Row 2 Knit.

Row 3 Purl.

Row 4 Knit.

Bind off, keeping last stitch on needle. Do not break yarn.

Turn the work, keeping the remaining stitch on the right-hand needle.

Back

With the last stitch on the bottom on your needle, pick up and knit 39 stitches along the bound-off edge. 40 stitches.

Row 1 Purl.

Row 2 Knit.

Rows 3–28 Work 25 more rows in stockinette stitch, ending with a knit row.

Bind off, keeping last stitch on needle. Do not break yarn.

Turn the work, keeping the remaining stitch on the right-hand needle.

Top Flap

With the last stitch of the back on your needle, pick up and knit 39 stitches along the bound-off edge. 40 stitches.

Row 1 Purl.

Row 2 Knit.

Row 3 Purl.

Row 4 Knit.

Row 5 Purl.

Row 6 (Slip1, k1, psso) 2 times, k32, (k2tog) 2 times. 36 stitches.

Row 7 Purl.

Row 8 (Slip1, k1, psso) 2 times, k28, (k2tog) 2 times. 32 stitches.

Row 9 Purl.

Row 10 (Slip1, k1, psso) 2 times, k24, (k2tog) 2 times. 28 stitches.

Row 11 Purl.

Row 12 (Slip1, k1, psso) 2 times, k20, (k2tog) 2 times. 24 stitches.

Row 13 Purl.

Row 14 (Slip1, k1, psso) 2 times, k16, (k2tog) 2 times. 20 stitches.

Row 15 Purl.

Row 16 (Slip1, k1, psso) 2 times, k12, (k2tog) 2 times. 16 stitches.

Row 17 Purl.

Bind off.

Tie

Transfer the stitches from your stitch holder to one of your DPNs. Reattach yarn and work I-cord (see Techniques section) for 5 in/13 cm. Bind off.

Double the I-cord over to form a loop and sew the end securely to the front panel right next to where your I-cord begins.

Assembling

Weave in ends.

Fold bag so that the top of the front and the top of the back are aligned. Use yarn needle and yarn to sew sides of bag using a flat seam. (See Techniques section.) When you get to the bottom, take care to square up the bottom corners with the edge of your side seam.

Felting

Felt according to instructions in the Techniques section. Since this piece is smaller, it's a great item to felt by hand. If felting by machine, check on it frequently to make sure the front and back of your bag don't felt together and that the I-cord loop remains open.

Pull into shape and lay flat to dry.

Finishing

Once the piece is dry, attach the button to the center of your top flap. You can use either yarn or thread depending upon the fixture of your button.

18

Concentric Circles Barrette

Embellished barrettes are great to have in your beauty arsenal. As someone who juggles a household, family, and career, I am not ashamed to tell you that I rarely, if left to my own devices, spend more than twenty seconds on my hair. On a good day, it gets washed and thrown into a ponytail. Therefore it's important to me to have an array of hats and hair doodads on hand to create the illusion that I've actually paid attention to my own grooming.

I adore the simplicity and perfection of a circle. It is an ancient symbol that manages to remain modern and chic. Many of my designs begin with this simple shape as a base, and here I pay homage to my muse, the circle. Hopefully, when worn, it will distract the casual observer from noticing I'm still wearing slippers.

* * * * *

Concentric Circles Barrette

YOU WILL NEED

Scraps of felted wool in various colors
See Upcycled Ornament pattern for suggestions.
Circle templates in 3 sizes
I used a shot glass, a quarter, and a penny.
Fabric marker
Sharp scissors
Needle and thread
Glue gun
4-in/10-cm barrette backing

* * * * *

To Make Up

Step 1 Using your templates, trace circles onto your felt, making 3 of each size.

Step 2 Cut out circles.

Step 3 Make 3 separate stacks out of your circles with the largest circles on the bottom and the smallest on top.

Step 4 Using needle and thread, sew each set of circles together using tiny stitches through the center.

Step 5 Use a hot glue gun to attach circles to barrette so that they slightly overlap.

19

Bangles

When my husband and I were approaching our first
wedding anniversary, I decided that I'd like gold bangles
to commemorate the important occasions in our lives.
My thinking was that someday I would be a wrinkled old
lady with an armful of glamorous bangles to represent
my favorite memories. So far I have four. In the meantime,
I thought it would be fun to knit and felt a few extra
bangles. These are perfect for winter—they are warm
and really brighten up a gray, dreary day. I love wearing
them with all black to add a striking splash of color.
Stack them together or wear them one at a time. These
knit up quickly and make a stylish, unique gift.

* * * * *

Bangles

SIZING

The pattern as written is for an average-size woman's wrist. It can be easily adapted for larger or smaller wrists by simply adding or subtracting a few stitches from the number you cast on.

GAUGE

10 stitches = 2 in/5 cm

YOU WILL NEED

Blue Sky Alpacas Sport Weight Yarn (100% baby alpaca; 110 yd/100 m per 50 g): 1 skein each in the following colors: Buttercup, Tangerine, Navy Blue, and Eggplant

You can substitute another luxury sport weight (#3) feltable yarn. You will need approx. 50 yd/45 m per bangle.

1 set US size 5/3.75 mm DPNs, or size to obtain gauge

Stitch marker

Yarn needle

Plastic grocery bag or other scrap plastic

Safety pin

Bamboo fiberfill or polyfill

I prefer the bamboo for sustainability and softness.

* * * * *

Knitting

Using DPNs and your first color, cast on 44 stitches.

Divide stitches evenly over 3 needles (15, 15, 14).

Pm after last stitch and join to knit in the round. (See Techniques section.)

Knit even for 24 rows.

Bind off.

Break yarn leaving an 18-in/45-cm tail.

Finishing

Fold the tube in half with cast-on and bound-off edges together and the right side facing out.

Thread tail through your yarn needle and sew sides together using a flat seam, leaving a 2-in/5-cm opening.

Cut a piece of your plastic bag to a size that can be pulled through your bangle. A 4-by-12-in/10-by-30-cm piece should do the trick.

Attach a safety pin to the plastic and pull it through the opening in your bangle; tie the ends together. This will keep the inside of your bracelet open during felting so it can be stuffed later.

Repeat these steps for each color of bracelet you make.

Felting

Felt according to the instructions in the Techniques section. It's best to felt each bangle individually by hand or in separate bags by machine so the colors don't blend.

Wring out excess water.

Remove plastic bags.

Stretch bangles over a soup can (or something of comparable size) to shape until dry.

Stuffing

Stuff each bangle with fiberfill and sew closed with sharp yarn needle and matching yarn.

20

Cat Ears Hat

What is there really to say about a cat hat? Do you have one? Probably not. Do you need one? Yes, yes, I think you do. I first made a miniature version of this hat for my daughter when she was a baby. Everyone thought she looked adorable in it. Strangers just couldn't get enough of an infant in a cat hat. Not to be outdone by my own child, I immediately set about making one for myself. You should have a cat hat in your wardrobe, too. It will add some whimsy to your days and also keep your ears toasty warm. Not to mention its usefulness in scaring off any marauding mice that might cross your path.

* * * * *

Cat Ears Hat

SIZING

This hat is knit to fit an average-size woman's head. It can be felted less for a larger size or more for a smaller size.

GAUGE

5½ stitches and 9½ rows = 2 in/5 cm

YOU WILL NEED

Patons Classic Wool Roving (100% wool; 120 yd/109 m per 100 g): 2 skeins in Orchid *or substitute 200 yd/190 m of any chunky weight (#5) 100% wool*

1 pair size 10.5/6.5 mm needles, or size to obtain gauge

Yarn needle

Stitch holder

* * * * *

Body of Hat

You will begin knitting from the top, or the "ears," of the hat. The hat is knit flat and seamed at the end.

Cast on 64 stitches.

Rows 1-6 Work even in stockinette stitch, beginning with a knit row.

Row 7 (K13, k2tog, k2, k2tog tbl, k13) 2 times. 60 stitches.

Row 8 Purl.

Row 9 Knit.

Row 10 Purl.

Row 11 (K12, k2tog, k2, k2tog tbl, k12) 2 times. 56 stitches.

Rows 12-16 Work even in stockinette stitch.

Row 17 (K12, kfb, k2, kfb, k12) 2 times. 60 stitches.

Row 18 Purl.

Row 19 (K5, kfb, k3, kfb, k5) 4 times. 68 stitches.

Row 20 Purl.

Row 21 (K5, kfb, k5, kfb, k5) 4 times. 76 stitches.

Row 22 Purl.

Row 23 (K6, kfb, K5, kfb, k6) 4 times. 84 stitches.

Row 24 Purl.

Rows 25-30 Work even in stockinette stitch.

Row 31 K2tog, knit to last 2 stitches, k2tog tbl. 82 stitches.

Rows 32–36 Work even in stockinette stitch.

Row 37 K2tog, knit to last 2 stitches, k2tog tbl. 80 stitches.

Rows 38–42 Work even in stockinette stitch.

Row 43 K2tog, knit to last 2 stitches, k2tog tbl. 78 stitches.

Rows 44–46 Work even in stockinette stitch.

First Earflap

Row 47 Break off yarn and place the first 28 stitches onto stitch holder. With right side facing, rejoin yarn to the remaining stitches, bind off 22 stitches, knit to end of row. 28 stitches.

Row 48 Purl.

Row 49 Knit to last 3 stitches, k2tog tbl, k1. 27 stitches.

Row 50 Purl.

Row 51 Knit to last 3 stitches, k2tog tbl, k1. 26 stitches.

Row 52 Bind off 6 stitches purlwise, purl to end of row. 20 stitches.

Row 53 Knit.

Row 54 and following even rows Purl.

Row 55 Knit.

Row 57 K8, k2tog tbl, k2tog, k8. 18 stitches.

Row 59 Knit.

Row 61 K7, k2tog tbl, k2tog, k7. 16 stitches.

Row 63 K6, k2tog tbl, k2tog, k6. 14 stitches.

Row 65 K5, k2tog tbl, k2tog, k5. 12 stitches.

Row 67 K4, k2tog tbl, k2tog, K4. 10 stitches.

Row 69 K3, k2tog tbl, k2tog, K3. 8 stitches.

Row 71 (K2tog tbl) 2 times, (k2tog) 2 times. 4 stitches.

Row 72 Bind off purlwise.

Second Earflap

Slip the 28 stitches from your stitch holder back onto needle. With right side facing, rejoin yarn.

Row 1 Knit.

Row 2 Purl.

Row 3 K1, k2tog tbl, k to end. 27 stitches.

Row 4 Purl.

Row 5 K1, k2tog tbl, k to end. 26 stitches.

Row 6 and following even rows Purl.

Row 7 Bind off 6 stitches, k to end. 20 stitches.

Row 9 Knit.

Row 11 K8, k2tog tbl, k2tog, k8. 18 stitches.

Row 13 Knit.

Row 15 K7, k2tog tbl, k2tog, k7. 16 stitches.

Row 17 K6, k2tog tbl, k2tog, k6. 14 stitches.

Row 19 K5, k2tog tbl, k2tog, k5. 12 stitches.

Row 21 K4, k2tog tbl, k2tog, k4. 10 stitches.

Row 23 K3, k2tog tbl, k2tog, k3. 8 stitches.

Row 25 (K2tog tbl) 2 times, (k2tog) 2 times. 4 stitches.

Row 26 Bind off purlwise.

Finishing

Weave in ends with yarn needle. Fold work in half. Using a flat-seam technique (see Techniques section), sew up the side of your hat. Turn hat right side out and fold so that seam is at center back. Use an overcast stitch to sew the top edges together.

Felting

Pay special attention to your hat while it's felting, as this type of yarn felts rather quickly. If felting by machine, check often during the wash cycle so as not to overshrink. I like this hat with a bit of pliability and think it's best if only lightly felted with stitches still visible.

Shaping

Hat can be laid flat to dry and will conform to the shape of the wearer's head.

21

Chic Hand Warmers

My hands are almost always cold, as I seem to come from a long line of "cold hands, warm heart" types. As an avid knitter, I can't wear gloves, because I need to be able to feel the fibers I'm working with and manipulate the yarn. Luckily these wrist warmers will keep your hands cozy while freeing up your fingers to get stuff done. And they look pretty cute, too.

* * * * *

Chic Hand Warmers

SIZING

Women's XS/S (women's M/L)

GAUGE

7.5 stitches and 9 rows = 2 in/5 cm

YOU WILL NEED

Cascade Yarn Lana d'Oro Paints (50% alpaca, 50% wool;
219 yd/200 m per 100 g): 1 skein in color 9923 (or 110 yd/100 m
of other worsted weight wool/alpaca blend) *or substitute
110 yd/100 m any worsted weight (#4) 100% wool*

US size 8/5 mm needles, or size to obtain gauge

Yarn needle

NOTE:
*You will make your wrist warmers in 4 separate pieces,
2 tops and 2 bottoms.*

* * * * *

Top (make 2)

Cast on 64 (80) stitches.

Row 1 *K2tog, repeat from * to end of row. 32 (40) stitches.

Row 2 *P2tog, repeat from * to end of row. 16 (20) stitches.

Work in stockinette stitch, starting with a knit row, for 11 in/28 cm more.

Bottom (make 2)

Cast on 16 (20) stitches.

Work in stockinette stitch, starting with a knit row, for 11 in/28 cm.

Finishing

Take one top and one bottom for each warmer, placing wrong sides together. Pin the bottom to the top just below the ruffle. Using yarn needle and a flat seam, sew edges of left side together on first warmer and edges of right side together on the second warmer.

On remaining open edges measure 3.5 in/9 cm from the top edge of the bottom piece (the piece without the ruffle), and place a straight pin here for a marker. Using a flat seam, sew from the bottom of warmer up to this marker, leaving 2.5 in/6.5 cm open for thumb, and then sew remainder of seam.

Felting

Felt your wrist warmers according to instructions in the Techniques section. This yarn felts pretty quickly and is a great project to felt by hand.

Lay flat to dry.

22

Cashmere Cuff

Nothing says luxury to me like cashmere. The feel of
it against bare skin is at once lavish and comforting. I
remember the first cashmere sweater I owned—it was an
olive green V-neck and at the time the most extravagant
item I'd ever purchased for myself. I loved that sweater!
This wrist cuff is a little piece of luxury you can wear
every day. Cashmere felts absolutely beautifully and lasts
a long time—just keep it away from pesky moths.

* * * * *

Cashmere Cuff

GAUGE

8 stitches and 9 rows = 2 in/5 cm

YOU WILL NEED

Trendsetter Kashmir Yarn (65% cashmere, 35% silk;
110 yd/100 m per 50 g): 1 skein in Plum (C1) and 1 skein in Gray (C2)
or substitute similar worsted weight (#4) cashmere blend yarn

US size 7/4.5 mm needles, or size to obtain gauge

Cotton string or yarn

Leather cord or ribbon

* * * * *

Knitting

Cast on 27 stitches in C1.

Row 1 Knit.

Row 2 Purl.

Rows 3–14 Work even in stockinette stitch.

The next 2 rows will create the eyelets you will use to thread your cord or ribbon through.

Row 15 K2tog, yo, k2tog, k19, k2tog, yo, k2tog.

Row 16 P1, (p1, k1) in yo, p21, (p1, k1) in yo, p1.

Row 17 Switch to C2 and knit.

Row 18 Purl.

Rows 19–32 Work even in stockinette stitch.

Bind off.

Felting

Thread cotton string or yarn through eyelets and tie in a knot. This will keep your eyelets from felting closed. Felt according to instructions in the Techniques section. Lay flat to dry.

Finishing

Cut cotton string from eyelet holes and thread the holes through with ribbon or leather cording. Tie to secure.

23

Rose Brooch or Barrette

This pretty little rose instantly adds interest and color to a drab lapel or hat. When worn as a barrette, it can turn an everyday ponytail into a work of art. Combine the flower with the cloche hat on page 145 and you've got a real showstopper.

The rose knits up quickly, but that doesn't mean that it won't impress. These make a fabulous gift that will have people saying, "I can't believe you made that!" It will be our little secret how simple it is.

* * * * *

YOU WILL NEED

Patons Classic Wool Roving (100% wool; 120 yd/109 m per 100 g): 1 skein in Orchid and 1 skein in Leaf *or substitute any chunky weight (#5) 100% wool*

US size 11/8 mm needles

Yarn needle

Flat-back pin bar or barrette backing

Glue gun

* * * * *

Rose

Cast on 12 stitches.

Row 1 Knit.

Row 2 and all even rows Purl.

Row 3 Kfb across. 24 stitches.

Row 5 Kfb across. 48 stitches.

Row 7 Kfb across. 96 stitches.

Row 9 Kfb across. 192 stitches.

Bind off.

Break yarn, leaving a 12-in/30-cm tail.

Leaves (make 2)

Cast on 3 stitches.

Row 1 Knit.

Row 2 and all even rows Purl.

Row 3 Kfb, k1, kfb. 5 stitches.

Row 5 Kfb, k3, kfb. 7 stitches.

Row 7 Kfb, k5, kfb. 9 stitches.

Row 9 Knit.

Row 11 Ssk, k5, k2tog. 7 stitches.

Row 13 Ssk, k3, k2tog. 5 stitches.

Row 15 Ssk, k1, k2tog. 3 stitches.

Bind off.

Finishing

Starting at one end of rose piece, begin to wind the piece around itself to create the rose shape. Thread tail through a yarn needle and sew into the rose to secure its shape. Weave in ends.

Felting

Felt leaves and rose separately. Once you've achieved the desired amount of felting, pull your pieces into shape and lay them flat to dry. Once dry, use a sharp yarn needle to sew leaves into place.

Making Up

Using a glue gun, attach your rose onto the pin bar or barrette backing.

24

Cloche Hat

I've always loved the fashion of the 1920s—the Charleston,
cigarette holders, bobbed hair, red lipstick, and kohl-rimmed
eyes all appeal to my inner flapper—to me they are the pinnacle
of feminine glamour. But my all-time favorite look from this
era is the iconic cloche hat. I love everything about a cloche.
I adore the way it couches the wearer in mystery, keeping
the eyes in shadow and showing off pouty lips. I also
love the fact that the domed top adds a bit of height to my
5-foot-2-inch frame. In my opinion, a cloche can make
anyone look and feel just a bit more elegant than usual.

* * * * *

Cloche Hat

SIZING

This hat is designed to fit an average-size woman's head. A custom fit can be achieved during felting and subsequent shaping.

DIMENSIONS

Circumference at widest point: 35 in/89 cm before felting; 27 in/68.5 cm after felting

Height: 13.5 in/34 cm before felting; 9 in/23 cm after felting

GAUGE

4 stitches and 5½ rows = 2 in/5 cm with yarns held together

YOU WILL NEED

Cascade Jewel Hand Dyed Yarn (100% wool; 142 yd/131m per 100 g): 1 skein in color 9284

Patons Classic Wool Roving (100% wool; 120 yd/109 m per 100 g): 1 skein in Gold *or substitute two chunky weight (#5) yarns*

US size 15/10 mm circular needle 24 in/60 cm long, or size to obtain gauge

1 set US size 15/10 mm DPNs

Yarn needle

Stitch marker

NOTE:
You will start knitting on a circular needle; switch to DPNs when you have too few stitches to continue on a circular needle.

* * * * *

Brim

With both yarns held together, CO 70 stitches to a circular needle. Pm and join to knit in the round. Work even in stockinette stitch until piece measures 3.5 in/9 cm.

Next row: (K2tog, k15) 3 times, k2 tog, k17. 66 stitches.

Bind off.

Crown

Pick up and knit 66 stitches from the inside (WS) of bound-off edge. This will create the welt detail around the brim.

Rounds 1-6 Knit.

Round 7 *K2tog, k9, repeat from * to end of round. 60 stitches.

Round 8 and all even rows Knit.

Round 9 *K2tog, k8, repeat from * to end of round. 54 stitches.

Round 11 *K2tog, k7, repeat from * to end of round. 48 stitches.

Round 13 *K2tog, k6, repeat from * to end of round. 42 stitches.

Round 15 *K2tog, k5, repeat from * to end of round. 36 stitches.

Round 17 *K2tog, k4, repeat from * to end of round. 30 stitches.

Round 19 *K2tog, k3, repeat from * to end of round. 24 stitches.

Round 21 *K2tog, k2, repeat from * to end of round. 18 stitches.

Round 23 *K2tog, k1, repeat from * to end of round. 12 stitches.

Round 25 *K2tog, repeat from * to end of round. 6 stitches.

Finishing

Cut yarn leaving a 10-in/25-cm tail. Using a yarn needle draw the tail through the remaining 8 stitches. Pull tightly and secure. Weave in all ends on wrong side of cloche.

Felting

Felt according to instructions in the Techniques section. If felting by machine, keep close watch on your cloche so that the brim doesn't curl up. This hat looks and feels best if you can still see some stitch definition. This yarn combination felts quickly, and overfelting will result in a super dense, too-small hat, so check frequently.

Shaping

To achieve the domed shape of the cloche, dry over a bowl in the appropriate size.

25

Baby Acorn Hat

If you have ever said to yourself, "How could my baby possibly be any cuter than she already is?" try this— make her an acorn hat! This little cap is simply irresistible on a baby. Best of all, the project knits up quickly and easily and makes a darling baby gift.

* * * * *

Baby Acorn Hat

SIZING

The size given will fit 0–6 months. Much of the sizing can be determined in the felting. If hat is too big, just felt it a little more.

GAUGE

7 stitches = 2 in/5 cm

YOU WILL NEED

US size 10/6 mm circular needle 16 in/40 cm long, or size to obtain gauge

Cascade Eco+ Yarn (100% wool; 478 yd/441 m per 250 g): 1 skein in color 2452 (MC) and 1 skein in color 9459 (CC) *or substitute 100 yd/90 m in chunky weight (#5) green wool (MC) and 50 yd/46 m in chunky weight (#5) brown wool (CC)*

1 set US size 10/6 mm DPNs

Stitch marker

Yarn needle

* * * * *

I-Cord

Using CC and DPNs, cast on 3 stitches. Make an I-cord 3 in/7.5 cm long. (See Techniques section.) Break yarn, leaving a 12-in/30-cm tail. You will use the tail to sew your "stem" to the top of your hat. Set aside.

Body of Hat

Using MC and circular needle, cast on 64 stitches. Pm and join to knit in the round.

Rounds 1-28 Knit.

Crown

Round 29 Switch to CC. *K1, p1, repeat from * to end of round.

Round 30 *P1, k1, repeat from * to end of round.

Rounds 31-32 Repeat rounds 29 and 30.

The next row will begin your decrease rows. Switch to DPNs when it becomes difficult to continue knitting on a circular needle.

Round 33 *K2tog, k6, repeat from * to end of round. 56 stitches.

Round 34 and all subsequent even rows Knit.

Round 35 *K2tog, k5, repeat from * to end of round. 48 stitches.

Round 37 *K2tog, k4, repeat from * to end of round. 40 stitches.

Round 39 K2tog, k3, repeat from * to end of round. 32 stitches.

Round 41 K2tog, k2, repeat from * to end of round. 24 stitches.

Round 43 K2tog, k1, repeat from * to end of round. 16 stitches.

Round 45 (K2tog) 8 times. 8 stitches.

Finishing

Break yarn leaving a 12-in/30-cm tail. Using yarn needle, thread tail through remaining stitches. Pull tightly and secure. Sew back and forth neatly across hole to cover, and weave in ends on wrong side of hat. Attach I-cord to center top of hat using yarn needle.

Felting

Felt according to instructions in the Techniques section and allow hat to dry on a bowl to create shape.

Resources

Thanks so much to all of the amazing companies that generously contributed yarn for the projects in this book. You can find them all at your local yarn stores or online.

Blue Sky Alpacas
www.blueskyalpacas.com
(888) 460-8862 Canada/
    North America
763-753-5815 International

Cascade Yarns
www.cascadeyarns.com
1224 Andover Park E.
Tukwila, WA 98188
(800) 548-1048

Classic Elite Yarns
www.classiceliteyarns.com
122 Western Avenue
Lowell, MA 01851
(978) 453-2837

Dr. Bronner's Magic Soaps
www.drbronner.com
P.O. Box 28
Escondido, CA 92033
(877) 786-3649

Lion Brand Yarn Company
www.lionbrand.com
135 Kero Road
Carlstadt, NJ 07072
(800) 258-YARN (9276)

Patons
www.patonsyarn.com
320 Livingstone Ave. S.
Listowel, Ontario, Canada N4W 3H3

Trendsetter and Naturally Yarns
www.trendsetteryarns.com
info@trendsetteryarns.com
(818) 780-5497

Index

Acknowledgments

When approached to write this book, I responded the way I do to most everything in my life: I said yes before considering the fact that I didn't really know how. So many people contributed to make the idea of *Heart Felt Knits* a reality. First and foremost is my editor, Laura Lee Mattingly, who brought me the idea in the first place. Her vision and gentle guidance turned this daunting undertaking into one of my proudest achievements. Chronicle Books took a chance on a first-time writer and provided me with the most amazing team. I owe a huge debt of gratitude to everyone at Chronicle, but especially to my art director, Ayako Akazawa, and to my technical editor, Kristi Porter.

I was so privileged to work with the most incredible photographers on this project, and I am indebted to Frank Ockenfels and Jessica Sample. They managed to see the vision I had in my head and turn it into a beautiful reality. I'm also lucky enough to have the two best friends in the world, and I couldn't have done this without either of them: Jennifer Laski, who found me incredible photographers, produced the photo shoots, and has always been my biggest cheerleader, and Christina Hendricks, my muse, trusted critic, and the most beautiful cover girl ever, inside and out. Thank you, my ladies.

Thanks also to Pearl Hanan for essentially managing my life *and* my career. And to my family, who has been extraordinarily patient with me during the writing of this book, I am forever in your debt. These people have dealt with a houseful of yarn, projects everywhere, my complete preoccupation with finding the perfect algebraic equation for every pattern, and my utter inability to commit to any plan: Diane Affourtit; Charlotte and Sergio Cascardo; Danielle Carr; John and Rosalina Mello; Lucas and Lisa Cascardo; and most importantly, my husband, Paolo Cascardo, and our daughter, Olivia. I love and adore you all, and I am eternally grateful that you continue to put up with me.